The Heart of A Military Leader

James Mr. Speaker Sears

Foreword by the late Dr. Hollis E. Pruitt

THE HEART OF A MILITARY LEADER

Email:
jamessears79@yahoo.com
Facebook:
http://facebook.com/james.f.sears
james.f.sears@facebook.com

Twitter: @MrSpeaker2u
LinkedIn: James F. Sears, Jr.
Instagram: @MRSPEAKER2U

Website:
http://www.jamesmrspeakersears.com/home.html

Publisher: Ms. Adrina Smith
www.mscreoleness.com
poeticarousal@mscreoleness.com
Editor: Ms. Tammy Lynn Hysten, San Antonio, TX

DEDICATION

To the poets on the grind,
To you writers doing time,
To the 757 (VA) poets who helped me hone my craft,
To the Vox Imperium Crew from Stuttgart,
Germany with whom I wrote and laughed,
To my mother, my rock, because she
encouraged me day and night,
To my Savior and my family in you I see the light,
To the poets on Joint Base Balad Iraq who
initially inspired me to write,
To all you poets out there sharing your flows,
here are my words so let's grow!

Foreword

Even in a land dedicated to freedom of speech, it is possible for millions from all walks of life to remain voiceless and unheard. These include homeless, those trapped in utter poverty, the working poor, and the victims of urban violence. Regardless of your ethnic background, region, age, gender, or lifestyle, too many of the marginalized and forgotten, Americans remain shadow people.

In *The Heart of a Military Leader*, Lieutenant Colonel James Sears throws aside the veil of silence and guides us in an intimate exploration of human struggle. He reveals the terror, fear, and courage of warfare in distant lands and the equally terrifying struggles of intimate relationships, family life, parenthood, and one's responsibilities to and for others with the courage required to lead and learn on these often overlooked battlefields.

Most importantly, in *The Heart of a Military Leader,* Colonel Sears gives a new and unique voicing of the experiences and perceptions of those who have served a not-always-grateful nation in times of war. In doing so, he not only honors their service and sacrifice, but he reminds us to find or make room for their voices in our everyday lives.

The late Dr. Hollis E. Pruitt
Former Coordinator of American Literature
Coordinator of Creative Writing
Thomas Nelson Community College

The Poetic Content (Journey)

THE HEART OF A MILITARY LEADER

Introduction

This poem is dedicated to those who have served, those who are serving, and those who will serve this great nation, and to the backbone of the United States Army, the Noncommissioned Officer Corps!

From the Heart of a Military Leader

Have you ever stood strong when fear was all around?
I mean, did you actually stand tall while others fell to the ground?

Have you ever done what common sense said not to do?
Even when others ran and said, "Come on man, do not be a fool."

Has fear ever gripped you so tightly you had to concentrate
just to breathe?
I am talking about the kind of fear that brings even the strongest men down to their knees.

Have you ever had to remain calm and lead others to a safe place;
while fear was clouding your judgment and causing your heart to race?

Have you ever been so engulfed by fear that 48 hours passed without you missing a single beat?
Heck, I almost went three days on just two hours of sleep.

Have you ever thought this could actually be the last breath I take; because death was all around you
with no room for error, absolutely no room for a leadership mistake?
Have you ever been so frozen by fear that you just did

not know what to do?
I have, but I had to go on because 237 Soldiers were
looking at me to lead them through.

See, fear in the face of leaders could destroy the will
of many people;
while fear that goes un-faced could become
deadly and extremely lethal.

Ok, well have you ever had to give an order that even
you were afraid to carry out yourself?
I mean, a command so crazy you would not do it
for all the world's wealth?

Have you ever had to send someone out on a mission you
knew they may not complete?
That would be one of those nights were this leader did
not get any sleep.

Have you ever had to give CPR to someone who worked
for you?
Well, I worked on Specialist Sierra for over one hour but
he just did not pull through.

Have you ever had to carry the body of someone who saved
your life?
The whole time I was thinking, what in the world am I
going to tell his wife?

Have you ever had to tell someone that her loved one
was no longer alive?
Trust me, you can actually see her heart breaking through
the tears flowing from her eyes.

THE HEART OF A MILITARY LEADER

Have you ever stood over a person who was dead due to an order you gave?
Look, do not stand too close at the funeral because you might want to jump into his grave.

Have you ever had to stand before a grieving family? Yes, it is completely sad.
Their Soldier gave his life for his country and all I had to give them back was a U.S. Flag!

I am a leader of Soldiers because that is what I was called to do, and just for the record, I am not trying to prove anything to any of you.

Most people just do not understand a true combat Soldier, warrior, and leader.
Well, here are some insights for all you poetry writers and readers.

How did you feel when the World Trade Center fell, the Pentagon got hit, and those planes hijacked?
This leader was devastated! Thousands dead on my watch, and it was my job to prevent those attacks.

You really do not understand the sacrifices we have made for the armed forces.
Heck, I have missed birthdays, holidays, anniversaries, and been through a couple of divorces.

We learn loyalty, honor, and respect for the U.S., for government, and for freedom, but we actually fight for our fellow Soldiers, you would understand if you ever took the time to meet them.

So yes, I have faced fears for you and even for those that
act like complete jerks,

because failure is just not an option for me in my line of
work!

I am a descendent from kings, forced into slavery, then turned
into a Soldier so here is my quote,
"I fought for this country before I had the right to vote."

I am the Buffalo Soldier who fought the Indians and settled
the west.
Absent from those history books, it was my blood, sweat,
and hard work that helped build the U.S.

I bravely charged up San Juan Hill and was later discredited
in the press;
because racism would not let the world view me as this
nation's best.

I am that courageous hard working Sailor who signed up
at that local rally;
to learn I could only serve my country from deep in the
ship's galley.

I am the black flier who defied all odds to fly, fight, and win.
Well, you might have heard them say that I am one of
those Red Tail, Tuskegee Airmen.

I fought in all the U.S.'s conflicts to include two world
wars to stop global oppression,
but it was not until the Korean War when we
overcame segregation.

The media and the public want you to call me a hero,
but you treated my Vietnam brothers, those Soldiers,
like complete zeros.

THE HEART OF A MILITARY LEADER

Those Vietnam Warriors followed orders, fought with
honor, and had no regret,
but when they came home, they came home to your insults, no
cheers, just total disrespect.

Well, this leader has faced his fears through multiple wars in the
Middle-East.
So, I salute those Soldiers dealing with fear right now
because they allow us to enjoy reading poetry in peace!

Chapter I Mentoring
Let's Grow!

Cry Like A Man

Son, do not believe the hype some people are out there selling.
Listen closely to me because it is only the truth I am telling.

You will soon be a man, a leader, a father, a king with a crown;
but before you take your throne, there are some things you have got to put down.

As a leader, you must learn to excel under pressure and succeed through stress.
See, others will look to you for guidance as that is one of your many test.

Understand I am not against crying because it can relieve and cleanse the soul.
Even the Savior wept, but I need to teach you to cry like a man before I let you go.

Son, cry with your heart as your fellow man commits crimes and goes to jail.
Cry with your support for him as you gather money to post his bail.

Cry with your education as you learn good from bad and right from wrong.
Even cry with your verses if you decide to recite poetry, sing, or write songs to correct wrongs.

THE HEART OF A MILITARY LEADER

Cry for your children as you put in work daily for your seed.
Rarely should you call in sick because you
have responsibilities and they have needs.

Cry with your pants pulled up, your belt worn tight, as you
show you have high standards.
Cry with a daily shower, clean clothes, fresh breath, and
always display your table manners.

Cry with promptness as you control your destiny and your fate.
Remember son, always be early because to be on time is
sometimes to be late.

Cry as you learn your trade, get hired, and cry as you do your
job exceptionally well.
Learn to communicate so others can understand the stories
you have to tell.

Cry with truth, loyalty, honor, respect, and cry with your dignity.
Refuse to be a victim, and continue to teach others as you help
fight illiteracy.

Cry with your love, sweat, determination, commitment, and cry
with your patience.
Son, cry with your ambitions, and cry as you overcome all of
life's complications.

Cry as you pray for others and be happy with their success.
Even cry with your failures, but cry by always doing your very,
very best.

Cry with your knowledge and the intelligence you received from
those books you have been reading.
Remember, you will have to work twice as hard and do twice
as much just to stay even, so keep achieving.

Cry for those saints that prayed you through all of
life's many issues.
See Son, real men cry a lot, but we cry with our
actions as we rarely take time to cry into tissues.

THE HEART OF A MILITARY LEADER

Raising a Queen (Dedicated to Ms. Jaila Catherine Sears)

To my baby girl, how I love you so.
My princess, my future, you are connected to my soul.

1 September 2006 is the day our eyes met.
Yes, love at first site, I will never forget.

I have prayed and waited years to hold you in my arms and hands.
I cut your umbilical cord and that is how our relationship began.

Your protector, father, teacher, and cheerleader, see I saw the first breath you drew.
Understand this, I am the first man that loved you.

No other person's love will ever match my love for you, as it is pure as distilled water.
The strongest bond ever is that between a father and his daughter.

My heart was pounding, I was so nervous, but I was your first.
The first to hold you, kiss you, feed you, look into your eyes, and quench your thirst.
It was me who inspected you from head to toe along with the nurse.

Baby girl, I love you so much as you are a gift from my heavenly Father above.
I am raising you to be a Queen so receive this guidance from your earthly father with love.

THE HEART OF A MILITARY LEADER

You are a princess, a lady, so carry yourself with dignity and respect.
No loud talking or cursing in public, and your manners you should never neglect.

Never drink directly from cans or bottles no matter the cost,
and make sure you sit with your legs or ankles crossed.

Display integrity, confidence, honesty, and no matter the trial,
always keep your head about you and when things get tough, relax, calm down, and smile.

My heart, draw your strength and confidence from me as I pray God guides you through.
Remember, if God be for you then do not worry about those who stand against you.

You are a natural born leader, raised in love so lead others with your heart.
Always speak the truth, stand against injustice, show others love, and from God never depart.

Baby, make your father happy, graduate from high school and then go onto college.
Always remain open to learning and after graduation continue to seek more knowledge.

My princess, always keep your word and honor every pledge you make.
When you do not keep your word, it is the heart of your father you break.

THE HEART OF A MILITARY LEADER

Study whatever you want, do whatever you like, and when you start, do not ever quit.
Do something you are passionate about and above all, be great at doing it.

You come from a long line of strong, beautiful, African women, now mixed with Indian and White,
but your bloodline is strong, see, that is why everyone knows you to be my princess on sight.

You are named after your grandmother Catherine, my mother who raised me to be King.
You are a Proverbs 31 woman, and you baby girl are a good thing.

Baby, live life on purpose, do not stay on your phone, or glued to that computer screen.
Keep your head and eyes up and focused as I am raising you to be a Queen!

Prison Rules

The names in this particular poem have been changed to protect the guilty!

Back in the day there was a young man called Little Kevin, who lived in the hood.
No father, but plenty of sisters and brothers so he did some things that could have been misunderstood.

For protection he joined a gang.
To fit in he started to speak slang.

Kicked out of school because he liked to bang;
out late at night is where he liked to hang.

For money well crack he began to slang;
because robbery and murder, well they were not his thang,

Nor were they in his blood.
My man Little Kevin was just a common everyday street thug.

By sixteen he was the man and by eighteen he was a leader by natural selection;
had a baby on the way because he refused to use protection.

He was still living with his mother when he had his second kid,
but that was when he got popped and sent up the river to serve a ten year prison bid.

That first night, Little Kevin caught hell in the cell he was in.
He went from being the man to being someone's girlfriend.

Brutally gang raped, ass-salted, violated, modern slavery was what he faced.
He was forced to follow *Prison Rules* if he wanted to one day walk out of that place.

There were many rules he had to follow but I will only highlight three.
The first rule was Little Kevin had to sit down, absolutely no standing while he peed.

This may not sound like a lot but stay with me if you can.
Sitting down to pee sends a psychological message that you are not a man.

The second rule was easy to follow while serving time.
He had no possessions because Little Kevin's man told him, "What's yours is mine."

Everything Little Kevin owned belonged to his man.
His food, his clothes, and even his life, were in another man's hands.

But that third rule is the reason why I am standing here with my tongue wagging.
For the next ten years, Little Kevin was forced to walk around prison with his pants sagging.

Sagging pants, well that is like wearing a wedding ring while you are in jail.

It lets everyone know that someone already owns and controls your tail.

This also gave his man the ability to always see Little Kevin's butt,
and it gave him easy access when he wanted to get a nut.

For ten years Little Kevin lived like this so he would not be beat.
He followed *Prison Rules* until the day came when he was able to reenter the streets.

From street king, to jail house queen, and now he was actually a hood legend to the youth.
Little Kevin's prison lover was locked down for life so he would never be able to get out and tell the truth.

Little Kevin's body was free but his mind was still in prison as he was out on the streets bragging,
so he continued to sit down on the toilet to pee and he still wore his pants sagging.

The youth saw Little Kevin as a hero, role model, and legend who followed no rules,
so they copied his style, his sagging pants because it was perceived as being cool.

So when you see young people wearing their pants low, you now know the truth,
and you need to recognize the impact people like Little Kevin and his prison lover have on today's youth.

Fatherhood

Let me tell you about the greatest job you will ever have -
Fatherhood.

Once you take this ride, you actually never turn back.
It's a lifetime commitment, so you might as well unpack.

Fatherhood is priceless and no other work can compare.
Where else in the world can you get this much fan fare?

Daddy's home is what rings through the house once you
open the door.
Stampede with an outpouring of love; brace yourself
because here comes more.

Jumping on Dad's back is one of the favorite games for
the boys,
while the girls greet you with warm hugs and lots of
noise.

Nowhere else in life will you be called Dad forty-five
times in less than sixty seconds.
You better answer because kids will not stop beckoning.

As a father, you are the answer man and the ATM.
You are their protector, playmate, and the biggest
cheerleader for them.

You are the provider, you represent the standard, justice,
and you are the truth.
You are her first love and his first coach, the hero who
lives under their roof,

down the street, or maybe in another town.
Divorce the spouse but for the kids, you still need to come around.

Keep your promises, mark your words, because they will remember; play your God given role.
If you have baby girls, your other job is to keep them off the pole.

Keep your son out of jail; fatherhood is a blessing that brings both good and bad.
Life is hard for a child to navigate without the guidance, love, and support of their Dad.

When you pick up one side of a stick, you pick up the other side as well.
Fatherhood is not an easy job so do not judge parents; learn from them so you will not fail.

Support and protect their dreams be that father many wish they had.
That is right, the best job in the world is being a Dad!

A Note to Leaders

I believe one of the first things to leadership is followership, see.
Leaders should learn how to be effective followers before they lead.

I once heard a leader say these words one day,
"Effective leaders are extremely good at communicating and showing the way."

Effective communication is when a leader causes a subordinate to...
believe what the leader say and see in them because the subordinate knows the leader's words are true.

Many get management and leadership confused, so just listen.
Management works in the system while leadership works on the system.

Leaders, measure what you say, how you act, and please watch what you do.
You cannot always talk your way out of problems you have behaved yourself into.

Remember, what you do speaks much louder than anything you say.
Actions do speak louder than words; that is what I want to convey.

Subordinates, peers, and superiors may not listen to you, but everyone always watches the things leaders do!

I have served with and learned from America's finest
while protecting the red, white, and blue.
Power corrupts; and absolute power corrupts absolutely,
I have learned this is so true.

So respect and protect any position of authority or
leadership you get;
because one simple leadership mistake in this business
could cause major regret.

THE HEART OF A MILITARY LEADER

Fear

I have had an intimate relationship with fear;
a kinship that pledged me for a number of years.

I have slept in fear, woke up next to fear, and ran from
fear, until I was out of breath.
I hid from fear, cried over fear, and even walked through
the valley of the shadow of death.

I gave into fear because I allowed it to control me.
I lost battles to fear as I stood still while it punched holes in me.

Surrounded and hounded by fear I fought back.
Found myself standing toe to toe with fear in the pitch black.

Darkness of my imagination, no running, I stood strong and
tall; to realize I was actually afraid of nothing at all.

Now I control fear see, I face fear eye to eye,
and for some reason, fear just seems to pass me right on by.

I stand here today because I have conquered fear, but I still
get occasional visits throughout the year,
so I show my courage and fear just disappears.

When you read your Basic Instruction Before Leaving
Earth it states 365 times, "Do Not Fear," for what it is worth.

You will learn, fearing God is when you start to
become smart;
because God did not put the spirit of fear in our hearts.

THE HEART OF A MILITARY LEADER

Never run from fear see, I have learned that is just the wrong
thing to do.
It will smell you out and then wreak havoc on you.

My advice is to embrace and disgrace fear.
Get a companion if you like and face then erase fear.

Even get radical and chase fear.
Catch it, snatch it, and then lay waste to fear.

So what is your phobia? What is your fear?
What is artificially holding you back?
What are you afraid of and what gives you a panic or anxiety
attack?

I am here to deliver a message that is crystal clear.
You can use courage, friendship, or the Word to control
and conquer fear.

Invictus Remixed
(Invictus by William E. Henley)

*Original Poem is in italics –
*Translation/remix is in bold

Out of the night that covers me, Black as a pit from pole to pole,
Let me break that down real quick so you can understand,
the pole to pole, well that is actually your life span.

The night that covers, just listen up because I can explain,
that stands for all the unknowns about from where we
actually came.

I thank whatever Gods maybe, For my unconquerable soul.
I know there is a God and He put everything I need inside of
me.

You can chain this body but my soul will always be
unconquered and free.

In the fell clutches of circumstance. I have not winced nor cried
aloud.
Just stop all the complaining about you being too this or too
that,

before God decides to take what little you do have right back.

Under the bludgeonings of chance, My head is bloody but unbowed.
Yes, I have taken blows and even the blood has started to
flow, but I am still standing strong, not broken, heck, I am
actually ready to go some more.

Beyond this place of wrath and tears Looms but the horror of the
shade,

THE HEART OF A MILITARY LEADER

You may have troubles here while living this life, but past this life is the unknown, which could be filled with misery and strife.

But yet the minutes of the year, Finds and shall find me unafraid.
You can look at me today or you can look at me tomorrow.

I will face all comers with no fear and no sorrow.

It matters not how straight the gate, How charged with punishment the scroll.
I do not care how difficult the path, or if you are struggling to buy food.

I also do not care if the judge gave you nine years for something you did not do.

I am the master of my faith: I am the Captain of my soul.
When it is all said and done, where I end up is within my control.

I am the leader of my life, I am responsible for the destination of this soul.

*William Ernest Henley 1849-1903

Chapter II Militarily Poetic
(Let's Serve)

Soldier's In-Brief

Welcome to your new unit, happy to have you.
This team of Soldiers will serve as your family while you
are assigned here.

You are now amongst America's finest, the best the Army
has to offer.

We prove it every day: We stand strong, so others do not
have to.

Yes, you have to be a little crazy to work with these guys,
but from what I have heard, you will fit right in with us as
that is what makes this job great, it is not for everyone.

Look, I will be up front with you, friends die in our
business, so choose wisely.

Keep your head down, your eyes open, and your mouth
shut.

Learning is your primary responsibility because around
here, some lessons kill.

These guys to your left and right will watch your back,
they may piss you off, and they could save your life all in
a morning's work.

You are expected to follow orders and adhere to the
standards. If you have questions about something I have

told you to accomplish, do if first, and then ask your question.

Back talk could get you some wall-to-wall counseling.

It is my job to get you back home to your wife, your mother, your girlfriend, or your dog.

Keep your stuff together, write your family, and watch what you say to them.

Do not have your family calling Red Cross looking for you or the commander may get upset.

Take care of your weapon and make sure you know where to go if we are attacked.

Start your count down now; you have 364 days and a wake-up until you get out of here.
You may as well count forward for now.

So welcome to the team.

Get some rest, our days start at 0400 and I cannot tell you when they end.

You sleep right here, you eat there, and you take care of your personal hygiene over there. Any questions?
I did not think so...

War Starter

If you want to start the next war,
well, then just go ahead Congress and cut the military
some more.

Our enemies are watching and waiting on us to make a
mistake.
Then they will swoop in and all our freedoms they will
take.

Please stop cutting the military Congress. I hope you
listen.
Just because crime is down, does not mean you should
get rid of your home security system.

If the United States falls in war, "watch out," is all I would
say.
South Korea and Israel would be attacked the very next
day.

Because North Korea wants to take South Korea's
economic might,
while the Muslim Brotherhood and Hamas would kill
Jews on sight.

The Russians would burn London and the Chinese would
land here in force.
No one would come to help the United States, of course.

It is the long arm of the United States Military that keeps
many of these countries free.
That is the main reason why the United States has so
many enemies.

Fear of our military is why our enemies show respect,
but Congress keeps cutting troops and treating us with
such neglect.

No one loves a Soldier until the enemy is kicking in the
front door.
So Congress, I beseech you, do not cut the military any
more.

Military Justice

After a service member has been accused of an offense and is under investigation, the accused enters my office and I say...

I am LTC James Sears, Commanding Officer, 840th Deployment and Distribution Support Battalion, Camp Arifjan, Kuwait. I am investigating the alleged offense of sexual assault, of which you are suspected. Before proceeding with this investigation, I want to advise you of your rights under Article 31 of the Uniform Code of Military Justice or UCMJ.

You have the right to remain silent, that is, to say nothing at all. Any statement you do make, either oral or written, may be used against you in a trial by court-martial or in other judicial, non-judicial, or administrative proceedings. You have the right to consult with a lawyer prior to any questioning and to have a lawyer present during this interview. You have the right to military counsel free of charge. In addition to military counsel, you are entitled to civilian counsel of your own choosing at your own expense. You may request a lawyer at any time during this interview.

Do you understand your rights as I have stated them to you? Do you want a lawyer?
-YES: Ok, do not say a word, inform the JAG Officer, you are being investigated for sexual assault and I have the following evidence:
-NO: Ok. Even if you decide to answer questions during this interview, you may stop the questioning at any time. Have you already consulted an attorney about this matter?

-YES: Stop and go to yes above.
-NO: Then are you willing to answer questions? Do you understand you are free to end this interview at any time?

I am investigating a sexual assault claim made by Staff Sergeant Jones.
Do you know Staff Sergeant Jones?
Are you and Staff Sergeant Jones friends?
What is the nature of your relationship with Staff Sergeant Jones?
Describe your actions on the day in question.

The United States military does not condone any forms of sexual assault. Just about every service member incarcerated today was incarcerated by another service member. I am not sure what you have heard but if you are guilty of sexually assaulting one of my people, my objective is to give you the maximum punishment allowed under the UCMJ. I have confined individuals for writing bad checks, absent without leave or AWOL, fighting, being drunk and disorderly, stealing, and other lesser offenses. Anyone under my authority who intentionally assaults an individual within my command that I am obligated to protect and safe guard will not be tolerated and will not be allowed to serve and represent this country in any way. I need you to give me the truth, give me the complete story. Remember, giving a false statement could lead to additional charges under the UCMJ. What do you have to say?

THE HEART OF A MILITARY LEADER

Orders!

The word came today to all of us,
thirty thousand to Afghanistan within a few months.

We can do the mission; I will lead you through,
but right now look, I have some praying to do!

God, you know I have been here before,
but I have one request as we hit the door.

Three hundred souls will be with me on the ground.
Please God, just help me get them all home safe and
sound!

THE HEART OF A MILITARY LEADER

War Described

Blown up buildings, burned out towns,
destroyed bridges, large craters in the ground.

Mangled bodies on abandoned streets;
shoes without people, people without legs and feet.

Melted medal with smoke filled skies;
crying while helplessly watching as a friend dies.

Hospitals on overload,
while bombs in my head explode.

Children with their hands out;
children with no hands walking about.

Helicopters flying over two by two,
PTSD, shell-shocked I am so confused.

Headed for a crash dive;
killing to survive.

See War:
        makes eyes dark,
        hardens hearts,
        makes close people to you distant,
        causes you not to want to listen.

        Makes your hearing fade,
        gives you scars that will not go away,
        changes your views on life,
        causes me to appreciate things and avoid strife.

THE HEART OF A MILITARY LEADER

Gunfights, sleepless nights, horrible sights,
where I actually gave in and started to write.

Delayed flights in and out of the war zone;
will I ever get home?

Safe at home, going back no more,
God please help me get my mind off war!

A Soldier Speaks

A Soldier speaks when spoken to.
A Soldier acts when called to.

A Soldier leads and a Soldier works.
Too much to drink, and a Soldier may become a jerk.

A Soldier loves passionately.
Mess with a Soldier's family and you will get a visit definitely.

A Solider thinks, learns, and walks.
When it comes to action, Soldiers are not a lot of talk.

A Soldier hurts and a Soldier heals.
A Soldier loves and a Soldier kills.

In times of trouble a Soldier knows what to do.
So make sure you listen the next time a Solider speaks to you!

Man Down

I never actually heard the shot that put my friend K.D. down.
There was just too much going on with explosions all around.

I saw him hit the floor; blood, pain in his eyes, red,
my movements' swift as I caught him, and, "hang on," is what I said.

No one stopped but me, see, there was nothing that could be done.
Life just kept moving even though it was about to lose a son.

I held him tight like he was my own flesh and blood, see.
Maybe my presence could prevent that bullet from taking his life. Maybe my strength could help him breathe.

Weigh carefully what you say to someone who is about to die,
The last words he was going to hear and I did not want to say good-bye or worst lie.

You are going to be all right, help is coming, it's not that bad, we have been through worse, none of this was true.
We need you, I'm sorry, please do not go, this is bull shit, all of this was true.

Hang on, hang in there. Bleeding, pleading, rocking, crying, while dying and still lying.
How on earth can you have a good day when your boy is in your arms dying?

THE HEART OF A MILITARY LEADER

Blood flowed relentlessly as it mixed with uncontrollable
salty liquids from my face;
vision   fuzzy   but   battlefield   smells   painted   an
unforgettable vivid account never to be erased.

When someone dies, I was told the human body gets
twenty grams lighter as your soul departs from you.
Well, it has been 9,734 days since my friend K.D. died in
my arms and I know that fact is true.

I Killed A Man Today

I killed a man today,
as I kneel here to pray.

He tried to take my life,
which would have caused all kinds of misery and strive.

He did all he could to survive.
He tried to put me away.

Today I was the better person,
but tomorrow is another day.

Tomorrow I may have to do this thing again.
Tomorrow I may have to face this man's friends.

If I had to, yes, I would kill again,
so please God cleanse me of this sin.

I can still see his face as I pray.
Please God take that memory away.

Help me to understand the reasons why,
you allowed me to live, but by my hands this man should
die.

I pray and pray so hard to understand,
because today is the day I killed a man.

THE HEART OF A MILITARY LEADER

Saddest Day - In Memory of SFC Christopher Phelps

The saddest day of service was like none other.
It was the day I had to say good-bye to my fallen military brother.

Sergeant First Class Christopher Phelps was his name.
One of the best athletes I ever witnessed; his initial claim to fame.

The sun rose and birds sang the way they always do,
but from our ranks fell the one person who we all went to.

His spouse held strong throughout the entire service.
Stone faced she sat calmly, no movements, no signs of being nervous.

But when I handed her that folded American flag everything changed.
She broke down, screamed a cry I never want to hear again.

I held strong like a Soldier should even though my eyes swelled.
Well, then came the roll call and that is when my tears fell.

The sergeant took his position,
and called the squad to attention!

THE HEART OF A MILITARY LEADER

Staff Sergeant Aaron Anderson – Here Sergeant.
Sergeant Mark Martin – Here Sergeant.
Corporal Steven Smith – Here Sergeant.
Specialist James Johnson – Here Sergeant.
Private Kimberly King – Here Sergeant.
Private Timothy Thomas – Here Sergeant.
Sergeant Chris Phelps......silence could be felt throughout
the entire place.
Sergeant Chris Phelps......more silence as the first tear ran
down my face.
Sergeant First Class Christopher Phelps.

Now everyone knew Chris would not answer those calls,
but that is how the Army grieves when one in our ranks
falls.

After a long overnight fight and as a unit prepared for the
next mission,
leaders used the roll call to see who survived so calling
the Soldier's names became a tradition.

Massive crying by all as we realize the finality of this
event.
Our Soldier, friend, teammate, and family member to
heaven was sent.

Another Soldier, patriot, and servant paid the ultimate
price for freedom.
I pray one day I am blessed to get to heaven to see, greet,
and thank him.

The Convoy

Destination predetermined, the mission must be accomplished according to the boss.
Get the convoy through no matter what the cost.

Packing, loading, checking, then briefings hours before we start.
Everyone is focused, concentrating because there is no coming back once we depart.

All this must be accomplished as these are critical preparations.
In this place every convoy is a life and death situation.

Halfway through the route is when the first rounds came across my face.
Heck, I had no idea my heart could beat at that pace.

There was no turning back, see, the mission had to get through.
I looked up and everyone was looking at me to see what I was going to do.

Noise, bullets, screaming, equals total kayos all around me, which was my prospective.
Turn, position my people, and fight was my command directive.

When my fifty caliber machine gun opened up and entered the fight,
I have to admit, that was the sweetest sound I ever heard in my life.

THE HEART OF A MILITARY LEADER

Now the bullets were flying in only one direction.
The enemy silent, running, hiding, and diving for protection.

It was not long before I commanded the fifty caliber machine gun to cease.
All through the valley there was nothing but peace.

Mission accomplished, the convoy got through.
Equipment, personnel delivered, and downloaded,
but WOW, it was a long time before I was able to travel without having my weapon locked and loaded.

Thank you God for getting our souls safely through all those fired rounds.
I appreciate you allowing me to get my Soldiers home safe and sound.

There are still Soldiers trying to get through under fire and driving while trying to reload.
I stand here for them praying so they can remain focused on those dangerous roads.

Enemy Within

The enemy could be close to you because the enemy is within.
The media acts like the enemy; do not think the media is always your friend.

Those famous last words are clearly written on the board.
Nothing you ever tell the media is completely off the record.

That is right, nothing is off the record when you speak to the press.
They will stretch, pull, rearrange, and distort facts in order to impress.

Who gave you your opinion when Rodney King was beat to the ground?
The media caused riots when that verdict came down.

Who told you OJ was guilty of double murder back in the day?
See, the media framed your opinion before the court had the final say.

Who told the world about Water Gate, Monica Lewinsky, and Abu Ghraib?
Who also told you about water boarding inside of Guantanamo Bay?

The press told the world Soldiers burned Korans over in the Middle East, and this was true,
but prisoners of war wrote in and used the Korans to communicate illegally with each other, but for some

reason the media decided that part of the story should not reach you.

The press will break a story to make money and to raise its value or stock,
but some of those stories are reckless and have caused Soldiers to get shot.

Our enemies just listen to the American press to decide what they want to do;
because the press keeps no secrets as it tells our enemies the best ways to hurt me and you.

The press will tell you how to build a bomb, hurt civilians, or where we are most at risk;
while our enemies just sit back, watch, listen, and compile their hit list.

If you listen to Fox News then you will get the conservative Republican view,
but if you listen to MSNBC then you will get the liberal Democratic side of the news.

Because today, the media is completely bias, spreading fear is one of their directives.
You cannot completely believe what they say as making money is their primary objective.

So the next time you sit down and listen to the local or national news,
Do not be upset if when you walk away you are completely sad, afraid, and somewhat confused.

THE HEART OF A MILITARY LEADER

For You

I have done things one should not do.
I have walked through fire not for me, but for you.

I have bled, I have cried, and gone hungry for you.
I have traveled miles, lost sleep, and friends for you.

I walked through the valley of the shadow of death for you,
then jumped out of a perfectly good aircraft, yes, it is true.

I have gone without, I have given things up, I have studied, and I have trained.
I have eaten things I would never offer you, and some things I could not even name.

For justice, for hope, and to be accepted by you;
for equality, for freedom, for humanity, and because I believe in you.

I stood watch during some very dark hours for you.
Climbed mountains, crossed deserts, and even swam oceans for you.

I have hoped and prayed, dragons and giants I have slayed.
I raised my hand, took a stand, protected this land for you.

For the good of you, and for the worst of you,
for the rich, poor, and for the homeless too.

For those in prison doing time,
for those committing crimes.

THE HEART OF A MILITARY LEADER

I stood against the worst for you,
and for you who stood against me,
I still stood for you,

so you would have the freedom to protest me,
and if you do not like the United States then I suggest you
just leave.

I may not know you, but it is true.
I stood, I lead, I tried, and some died for you.
For you I served, for you, I Soldiered!

Garrison Combat

Let's do this once without multiple sequels,
bottom line, all men are not created equal.

Sometimes you may need to step back to regroup,
and you may have to shut down in order to reboot.

We are in a hole, Houston, we have a problem and it is a biggin,
so when you find yourself in a hole, the first thing to do is to stop digging.

Post traumatic stress disorder, shell shock, and war traumas are not pranks.
Suicide is claiming one active duty Soldier and twelve veterans per day from our ranks.

Service personnel stand tall and strong for freedom and not for greed,
so where are you while these warriors are in need?

Soldiers do not need your handouts, sympathy, or wealth.
Just give them a smile, thanks, compassion, and understanding as they deal with bad health.

So speak to and appreciate those Soldiers, Sailors, Airmen, and Marines.
They are a part of the reason why you have peaceful dreams.

Just let them know you appreciate what they do, because without them the world would see the fall of the red, white, and blue.

The Army and Me

Mama, mama, can't you see,
what the Army has done for me?
Stood me up and dressed me down,
marched me all over town.

Taught me right and showed me wrong,
ran my butt singing Army songs.
Hurry up and wait is what we do,
follow orders, or you are through.

Rain or shine we never stop,
lost all my hair at the barber shop.
Standing tall and looking good,
ought to be in Hollywood.

Workout before we see the sun.
Every day you know we run.
Got my orders and I am out the door,
flying to settle some political score.

The Army put me on an airplane,
calls me by my last name.
We stand, we hold, and we fight.
We always try to do what is right.

Leadership, discipline, and values too,
join the Army there is some for you.
So mama, mama, can't you see.
The Army has made a man of me!

Chapter III Biblically Poetic
(Let's Pray)

No Pride for Me

You may have heard it said, "Pride cometh before a fall,"
but I really do not think people understand what this means
at all.

If you truly understood, then you would not be proud of this
nor that;
wouldn't that actually mean your fall was coming next?

You also would not walk around with a proud look or
act certain ways,
and you would definitely change a lot of the things you say.

Pride is the number one thing out of seven that God hates.
Read Proverbs Chapter 6, verse 16-19, as this is a fact
and is not up for debate.

Here is a scene from the Bible where you will see no pride.
God looks down as His Son was being baptized.

God said, "This is my beloved Son in whom I am well pleased."
This is your lesson for today, so please listen closely to me.

God did not say, "Here is my Son, I am proud of what He has
done."
He was teaching us all a lesson through His very own Son.

Look, be proud of nothing, not children, self, friends, or
anything at all,
unless you want your pride to bring about your own downfall.

THE HEART OF A MILITARY LEADER

Pride has graveyards packed from end to end.
Pride is also listed as one of the seven deadliest sins.

Yes, pride really does come before a fall.
Check around because those who have learned this
lesson are not standing at all.

The world will tell you, "Showing pride is ok, and being proud
is all good,"
but be careful because it is the Bible not me they have
misunderstood.

Displaying pride takes ownership of what God has
accomplished in your life.
Give respect where it is due or you could bring about your
own misery and strife.

Yes, God is love, God is good, and remember God is great,
but do not forget, pride is still the number one thing the God in
my Bible hates!

THE HEART OF A MILITARY LEADER

Poetic Shepherd

The Lord is my poetic shepherd; I shall not have writer's block.
He maketh me to write on white paper or card stock.

He leadeth me beside the still waters and calm places.
He restoreth my ability to write words my heart and soul embraces.

He leadeth me down the righteous path writer's take,
yes, all for His name sake.

Yea, though I spit poetry in some of the shadiest places,
I will fear no evil hecklers who have no social graces.

For Thou words art with me;
Thou pen and paper comfort me.

Thou providth an open mic in restaurants, bars, or pubs.
Thou anointed my tongue with the grace of a dove.

So people listen while they drink and eat their grub;
as my poetic flows pour over everyone in the club.

Surely, poetic verses and vibes shall follow me all the days of my poetic life,
and I will dwell in the house of our Poetic Lord forever,
Yes that's right!

He Cried
(Inspired by Pastor Chris Konicki)

Listen up and I'll tell you why,
my Savior one day cried.
John Chapter 11 and the 35th verse tells it all,
and it is also the shortest verse in the bible ya'll.

He did not cry just because of the people's compassion,
and He actually did not cry to teach us a lesson.
He did not cry because Lazarus was dead.
Read the story again because that is not what it said.

See, my Savior has control over life and death.
He controls all, so investing in Him will give you eternal
wealth.
By the time my Savior reached Lazarus' side,
it had been four days since Lazarus had died.

He saw the mourners grieving as He passed by,
but their sorry and anguish is not why He cried.
See, Lazarus was in heaven which is the best place to be,
but to teach us a lesson, he had to be brought back to
earth, and that made my Savior grieve.

Just think you are in heaven with our heavenly Father at
complete rest.
Then you are summoned to come back here to all this
earthly mess.
Lazarus was safe in heaven at God's side.
Bringing him back to earth is the reason my Savior cried.

Touch Not!

In Chronicles and Psalm we are told, "Touch not my anointed ones," "Do my prophets no harm." After being told this twice in the Bible we still seem to get this wrong.

Touching someone does not always mean physically putting your hands on him or her.
Many of us touch people with our harsh and hateful words.

The Bible has examples, yes, lessons that should be learned and studied.
First, check out 2nd Kings Chapter 2 starting at verse 23, a tale that gets bloodied.

The anointed Prophet Elisha was mocked and called names by some young lads.
A group of young boys hurled insults at an old man which is completely sad.

Well, because that old man was a prophet, he cursed those boys in the name of the Lord,
and two bears came out of the woods, forty-two lads completely gored.

Verbal touching can be just as powerful as physical licks.
Stick and stones break bones and words hit like bullets or thrown bricks.
If you cast harsh words towards an anointed person, talk about them, or wave your fist, well, you could be hurting yourself and putting your life at risk.

THE HEART OF A MILITARY LEADER

Check out Shimei the Benjamite in 2nd Samuel Chapter 16 verses 5-8.
Shimei cursed King David and threw stones, but Shimei did not have his facts straight.

In the end, Shimei ate his harsh words.
His mouth signed a bad check.
He bowed to King David, and begged for forgiveness in order to save his neck.

People can do strange things and you may not completely understand.
Treat them with love because many spoke ill of Noah as he worked God's plan.

The power of life and death are in the tongue.
Words mean things so think before you release.
Words can kill, so speak love, kindness, health, wealth, and by all means speak peace.

Words can hurt or harm those they were directed to,
but do not forget your own words can come back and adversely impact you.

Words cut both ways while they are coming out or going in.
Measure and weigh all your words carefully; spell check before you hit send!

So, treat everyone like they are a child of the Most High as you really do not know.
The next time you speak ill of someone it could be your face getting cracked as it hits the floor.

Poetic Psalm

Recite joyfully your poem unto the Lord,
all ye poets in His lands.

Write to the Lord with gladness.
Know you are before His presence,
every time you take the open MIC.

Know everyone that the Lord He is God.
It is He that gave us the heart to write, not ourselves.

We are His poets,
his instruments of communication.

Enter His writing realm with thanksgiving,
and into open MICs be ready to praise His name.

Be thankful unto Him that you are His writer,
and bless His name when you write.

Writing for the Lord is good.
His inspired words last forever.

His truth is unwavering,
and will bless generations of poets and poetry lovers for
years to come.

The Fifth Commandment

We were given a commandment for what it is worth,
"Honor thy father and thy mother, so thy days may be
long upon the earth."

"Days long upon the earth," well that actually means a
long life.
Dishonoring your parents will shorten your days and
nights.

God's words have transcended time, and sometimes they
are misunderstood,
but what is interesting is the fifth commandment does
not include the word good!

You were not told to honor thy good father and good
mother, get it straight.
Your responsibility is to honor them because it is a
spiritual mandate.

To hold in high respect, rank, position, or one with great
privilege as it seems.
I know some are wondering right now what does honor
actually mean?

Poppa may have been a rolling stone.
Heck, momma may not have created a happy home.

You could have been raised like one of the Huckstables,
or you could have labeled your family as completely
dysfunctional.

Your father could have several kids outside his home,
or your mother could have been out in the streets getting
stoned.

I am telling you this now as I am pouring my heart out
tonight.
Dishonoring your parents may hurt them, but it will
shorten your life.

Do not stand in judgment of your parents regarding the
things they do.
Judging them could bring even more heartache back to
you.

Look, it does not matter if you have the worst parents in
the world.
God blessed them with you when you were a newly born
baby boy or girl.

Not forgiving; that is like taking poison into your own
body and hoping it kills someone else.
You must forgive, move forward, and let it go before you
destroy yourself.

You must honor your parents. That is more than a
request.
It is a commandment you will have to answer for at God's
bequest.

Look, the bottom line is, you cannot control the actions of
others.
Do your part and always honor your father and your
mother.

Believe It!

There are facts and information in books, but you will not read it.
There is oxygen in water, but you cannot breathe it.

There are different things in all fifty states, but this one, you will not leave it.
Even when someone finally tells you the truth, you do not believe it.

There are cautions posted on the roads, so you better heed it.
You could be headed for destruction, but cannot perceive it.

You may not believe in God, but what will you do when you first see Him?
Success and heaven are out there for you, but without hard work you will never achieve them.

You want a relationship, but you find it hard to conceive it.
You have so much old baggage, and you just cleave to it.

There is education for you in college, but you act like you do not need it.
Here are some facts, open your mind and heart, so you can see it.

Fact: Noah took seven of the clean animals on the ark not just two each! Read it again.

Fact: At the time of Jesus' death, crucifixions where carried out on trees or long wooden poles not crosses. Do some research.

Fact: When Jesus lived, there was no letter "J" in any language anywhere.

Fact: The letter "J" was invented in the Seventeenth Century, 1600 years after His death.

Deduction: When Jesus walked this earth he was not called Jesus. Do some research, and then come see me.

Fact: King James had the Bible re-written to spread the Christian religion to Europeans after the Jews and Africans had somewhat rejected Christianity.

If you do not believe what I have told you, open your mind and then explore it.
Do your own research; you should not just ignore it.

Set your goals so you can achieve Him.
Books have information so you may want to read them.

God created you; put you here to hear this, so I hope you receive it.
I have done my part because facts, knowledge, information you know, real stuff, I have just delivered it.

Prayer

In the Bible, your Basic Instructions Before Leaving Earth, we were taught how to pray for what it is worth.

We were taught to pray to our Father in heaven.
We were not taught to pray to rosary beads you can purchase at the Seven-Eleven.

We were also not taught to pray to manmade things or each other,
and we were not taught to pray to Mary, yes, our Savior's mother.

We were not taught to pray to the cross whether on your neck or in the ground.
The cross has no religious significance, and in the original Bible it cannot be found.

At the time of the Savior's death there were no crosses around.
He was crucified on a long pole or tree.
His feet nailed together; His hands over His head, together and bound.

King James and others decided to use the cross to symbolize the crucifixion.
They had the Italian Madonna sculpted so people would worship Mary, even more fiction.

We were taught how to pray in the New Testament book of Mathew Chapter 3.
You will see He did not mention hail Mary's, crosses, or even rosary beads.

Stop praying to those manmade idols unless you can find
it in the written word.
Direct all your prayers heavenly through the Son to God
if you want them to be heard.

Do not get upset with me. I am just the messenger.
Study and I pray you will see the light.
Prayer changes things, but you have got to be doing it
right!

Many good and bad traditions were taught, and some of
them need correction.
Remember, my God is a jealous God, so make sure you
are praying in the right direction!

Chapter IV Notes to Poets

Poetry Lover

Let these words reach you as from my lips they depart.
May they speak to you through your ears and penetrate
your heart.

Poetic love is what I want to tell you about.
The best I ever heard and that is no doubt.

It was a clear and cold night with poets preparing to spit
and spout.
I had no idea it was me she came to talk about.

She was slinging words from the left and from the right.
This was beautiful, but I had to remind myself this was not a
fight.

Her words were hitting me way below the belt.
Her poetry made me sweat as I looked around for some
help,

but there was none to be found as she spit verse after
verse.
I was so hot, but her words actually quenched my thirst.

She read me up and down; embarrassed I turned my
head trying to hide.
She said what I was thinking as her poetry crept up my
thighs.

She was right, I was guilty, but I asked for an appeal.
Her words spoke my life. I felt like Lauryn Hill.

Her poetry satisfied all my needs;
Pure pleasure, wow, verbal ecstasy.

At first I was nervous, but her smooth words caused my
fear to diminish.
I was straight; heck, I actually thought she was finished.

So I shook her off; gained my composure to mount a
verbal counter attack.
Then her words began to stroke me even more and
knocked me flat on my back.

I was down, but not out from the melodious words she
blew.
She stepped over me and said, "Mr. Speaker, I am not
through with you."

She waxed poetically for hours, as listening was all I
could do.
I was focused on her words; my eyes to her mouth,
completely glued.

I woke the next morning with her on my mind.
I was held captive by her words until 11:59

because at midnight she opened the door and grabbed
her coat.
That was all I remember before I awoke.

I arose with a smile, no hangover, but was last night for
real?
Yes, because her words were in my heart; even her
punctuation had sex appeal.

THE HEART OF A MILITARY LEADER

I searched, she was gone, but I found a note on top of the bed covers.
It read, "I will see you the first Thursday of the month at poetry night my lyrical lover."

I relaxed with a smile all across the front of my head.
Poetic loving was great anywhere because I never made it to the bed.

Poetry, WOW, who knew it would be so tight.
Well, keep reading because maybe you will get some poetic loving tonight.

Dear Poetry

Hello poetry I hope you are having a great day.
I have a confession to you that I must convey.

Poetry, you were not my first love, not my second, or my tenth either.
I was a hater of writing because I am not that great of a reader.

I avoided you all through my daily walk.
I would never pay attention whenever you started to talk.

I made excuses; called you derogatory names as I was afraid.
I was an athlete and poetry was for nerds, book worms, or gays,
but you never gave up on me and you always showed me love.
Finally, you floated into my life with the grace of a dove.

You taught me how to express myself in so many new ways.
You looked deep inside me as you knew I had so many things to say.

You showed me how to open up dark secret parts of my life.
You even helped me get over pain and disappointment brought to me by my ex-wife.

Poetry, you have befriended me, educated me, and even angered me as well.
You chased me, stalked me, woke me up, and hounded me because you knew I had stories to tell.

THE HEART OF A MILITARY LEADER

Poetry, you just take over my mind anytime night or day;
even while I am driving or in church or sleep because
from you I cannot get away.

I appreciate how you taught me that poetry is for all
people straight or gay;
because I have heard some of the erotic things poets
convey.

Thanks for helping me deal with my failures, grief, and
depression.
You allow me to write my feelings, grow, and reduce my
stress as I teach a few lessons.

Through you poetry I have been able to confront, teach,
and educate.
I have been able to enlighten, inspire, anger, help, and for
some even stimulate.

Poetry, you even know the pace of my pulse, and how I
get my daily start; you even know the condition of my
heart.

You know the people's poetic needs,
and you know how to make my pen bleed.

You know where ignorance needs to be taught.
You know where minds need to be brought.

I will do my part and tell stories that need to be told,
and poetry, you take real good care of my heart you now
hold!

Why I Write

I write things down because you may have missed them,
and then I speak them out with the hope you will listen.

I write because you need to hear the truth.
I write in order to give you proof.

I write because just about every song you ever heard
started out as a thought, and then became spoken word.

I write for freedom, to provide vision, to educate, and tell
the truth.
I write to enlighten, brighten, your day, and to inspire the
youth.

If you want to hide something from a black man, just
write it down.
Well, it's the ugly truth no matter how bad it sounds.

See black men, we have learning all wrong.
You cannot get all your education through rap music and
sex songs.

I write because we need to broaden our awareness and
knowledge.
I write to teach because some did not attend college.

You need someone to tell you how life is, and I am your
volunteer;
conducting mental surgery with no antiseptic through
your open ears.

If you want to hide something from a black man then just
put it in a book;

because I was told that is the last place he is going to look.

I know songs served as the primary educational tool for blacks back in time,
but this is a new day; things have changed, grow up, read a book, and expand your mind.

Reading and writing were beat out of us and incorrect, information was put in;
because reading and writing were perfected way back with the Egyptians.

That is right, study, research, and you will see
most of Europe and Asia learned at the early African's knees.
Then European invaders came to Africa on ships and boats, and stole most of the things those Africans wrote.

If you want to hide something from a white man,
start talking about race;
because sometimes pride keeps him from hearing you even if you are speaking directly to his face.

Prevent the black man's education was one of his overall themes in the community.
Over 260 years of slavery and people get upset after only fifty years of equal opportunity.

One more group has a story to tell,
if you want to hide something from a woman, place it right next to a shoe sale.

I write for my own liberation,
and to continue to improve my communication.

THE HEART OF A MILITARY LEADER

I write because of so much incorrect education;
because I actually learned more after my graduation.

I write because there are just so many things you need to
know.
Like my man Infinity says, "Let's grow."
Let's grow wiser together and educate each other.
I speak once I have researched, and new things I have
discovered.

Like the history of spoken word, about Little Africa, or
because some people are just not readers,
or about the First Cowboy, Buffalo Soldiers, or to tell you
what it is like to be a Military Leader.

I write because God gave me the gift of words,
and then sent me to college for an education, so that
more of you I could serve.
I do not really need to see my name up in lights,
but ever so often I long to speak via the open MIC.

I write because this is what God has commissioned me to
do.
I write because it is the best way for me to show my heart
to you. Read a book, I am begging you.

Do like Malcolm X did while he was doing time.
Educate the head, body, and soul,
and that could free your mind, and for some it could even
free your behind.

Poetry Junky

While attending a weekly meeting for individuals addicted to poetry, I say...
"Hello, my name is Mr. Speaker." – They say, "Hello Mr. Speaker."

I am addicted to poetry or this poetry drug.
See, I am a poetry junky.
It is on my back like a gorilla, you know, like a big ink monkey.

No poetry after forty-eight hours and I become an instant fiend; I go crazy spitting poetry anywhere like in my shower, or to guys who are already pushing up daisies.

Look for me out late at night getting my poetic fix.
Three places to check out on Monday nights, that does the trick.

I even listen and spit poetry on the radio.
I chase poetry like pimps chase crack noooooo.

If I do not put these words down on paper and then recite; I will not be able to get any rest, and I may be crawling in your window late at night.

Poetic movies, plays, and books,
open MIC, spoken word, now that is my hook.

I can just listen, you can read, or I can take the MIC, it is insane.
To listen or to be heard, I just need more poetry up in my veins.

THE HEART OF A MILITARY LEADER

Everything to me is poetry, give it to me and I will read,
smoke, or write it.
I hear real poetry only begins when true poets start to be
honest about shit.

I am the poet, and I am the explanation.
I am what it says, and I am also the clarification.

I give it to you correctly with no tricks.
I can even give you old poems with a little remix.

Damn right, I sleep with my pen, paper, laptop, and
notebook.
I get up the next morning with most of the poem written
even the hook.

Poetry to me is like hair to Sampson, like politicians and
votes, or water and boats;
like preachers and churches, like restaurants and food, or
like coffee needs to be brewed; like cars and gas, books in
class, yards with grass, knuckles and brass;

like news and weather, like birds with feathers; see me
and poetry, we just go together.
Hello, my name is Mr. Speaker, and I am a poetry junky!

If Poetry Was a Crime

If poetry was a crime, I would be wanted like Adolf Hitler,
or chased through Gotham City like the Joker and the
Riddler.

I would be operating underground like Harriet Tubman,
in and out of trouble while on a path straight to prison.

I would have a record as long as a roll of new two-ply
toilet tissue.
I'm never going to stop spitting man, forget you.

Look, if poetry was a crime, I would be public enemy
number two in no time ya'll,
right behind that idiot who made poetry against the law.

I would be America's most wanted and Mr. Speaker is not
what you would call me.
My new name would be inmate 65487423!

Even incarcerated you would not be able to stop these
words,
that would just make me have to memorize my poetic
flows to be heard.

And speak is what I would do until the day they shot me
or stabbed me with a knife;
which may kill me, but it would bring all my words to life.

Trying to stop poetry is like attempting to prevent water
from hitting the beach,
or it would be like trying to make T.D. Jakes not preach.

THE HEART OF A MILITARY LEADER

Poetry is my Bonnie and to poetry I am Clyde.
Poetry is the fuel in the cars I drive.

I am two parts hydrogen while poetry is one part oxygen;
combined we make water, so that means together we are
always flowing.

Flowing with the combinations of nouns, adjectives, and
verbs; always striving to give you something you have
never heard.

As a poet, writing is thinking and breathing which is
living, you see.
Take that away and you will see another side of me.

Making poetry a crime is actually an act of war, so with
me you have just made an enemy,
and that very day I will be kicking in your door.

I will kidnap your kids, slap around your wife, and even
beat your darn cat,
and when I find you, write your will because two to the
chest and one to the head is what you will get.

So do not mess with poetry if you know what is good for
you and yours.
If you do, then you can bet your last that we are going to
war.

Call me Al Capone, Jimmy the Kid, Big Meech, or Bumpy
Johnson if you prefer.
If poetry was a crime then I would be your new American
Gangster.

Put it There!

When times are hard and you feel like hurting someone,
calm down, relax, pick up your pen, and put those
feelings into a poem.

When friends come through for you and prove they are
really watching your back,
or when church folks gossip about you without even
knowing all the facts.

When a person you really want to meet smiles and gives
you a wink,
or when you make love and it feels so good you cannot
even think.

When all your plans seem to take a turn for the better or
the worse,
especially when someone steals money right from your
wallet or purse.

Do not stay angry or try and hurt them in any form.
Take a deep breath, count to ten, and put those emotions
in a poem.

When your boss is acting crazy, or when your check
comes up short,
definitely when your car will not start, and you have got
to be in court.

When you put all your money into an investment that
flops,
or when your team loses the big game on a last second
shot.

THE HEART OF A MILITARY LEADER

Even if you are dealing with depression and thinking about doing yourself in, stop! Take a minute, gather your thoughts, and pick up that pen.

Put your feeling in a poem when you are down and felling stressed.
Do not bury those feelings deep inside, get that mess off your chest!

Maybe you just realized you are in love and it is the best feeling you have ever felt,
or while playing cards you got ten spades in the hand you were dealt.

When a man you do not love publically proposes to you,
or when the elevator is out, you live on the tenth floor, and you have eight bags full of food.

Especially when your lover walks out on you once again,
or when there is more money going out then what is coming in.

When you catch a break, get a pay raise, or your favorite team wins,
or when your husband has dinner with two of your old boy friends.

Put it in a poem, bring it here, poetry will listen to what you have to say.
Poetry is uplifting; it will look you in the eyes and ease your pain right away.

Poetry is love, poetry is hate, and poetry can even be the blues.
Poetry can be freedom, prison, or it can be the medicine that actually cures you.

Tell poetry your success, your failures, or about that lover you are missing.
See, poetry is always available 24/7, 365, yes, poetry is there to listen.

I Love Poets

I love being in the company of poets.
People who tell it like it really is.

Story tellers, writers, speakers, communicators, and authors, are individuals who can make you cry, laugh, or think deeply.

Some use poetry to preach, while I use poetry to breech, gaps of ignorance, as I attempt to reach.

Then once I have your attention I will teach
through spoken word which is verbal speech.

Minds open,
heads down,
pens up,
words flowing,
brain storming,
sentences forming,
hearts warming,
poems informing,
people transforming,
while poets are performing.

There are fingers snapping, some are clapping, but no one is napping.

Dreamers dream, singers sing, and pilots take flight, when all else fails put me in the company of poets who think and write.

Chapter V Historically Poetic

History of Spoken Word

In the beginning there was the Word and that Word was spoken.
The simple combination of words, and this world as we know it was awoken.

From Africa, through the Middle-East, Europe, Asia, the Word touched many places.
Different languages, cultures, creeds, colors, all of them the Word embraces.

Overtime Spoken Word became dialogues, monologs, and speeches.
Later Word grew into plays, movies, and even storytelling, history teaches.

Once Spoken Word was joined with music they formed a lasting combination,
providing lyrical enjoyment, exhilaration, and for some, complete relaxation.

From poetic rhythmic word patterns, to celebratory combinations,
to religious renditions to today sexual gyrations.

Spoken Word is the source from which all things flow.
Thoughts form in the brain and out of the mouth they must go.

THE HEART OF A MILITARY LEADER

That is if you want your thoughts to ever take form or flight.
Some have to put words on paper to edit and then later they will recite.

Writing is freedom, it is revolutionary, and it is a way to relieve and release stress.
True writing is fearless, full of expression, because it is completely boundless.

To you poets, my people, here is my prayer I am sending through,
may similes slide off your tongue and may your metaphors melt those listening to you.

May your rhymes ripple, as you harden nipples, while hitting verbal triples, and home-runs.
May your tongue never be forked and your words never twisted or bit.
May you always receive finger snaps while you spit.

So, shout out to all you true writers reading this right now.
I know you carry words in your head like passengers until you right them down.

Once those thoughts are put on paper it is like your mind has been released;
that is the very first time a writer can finally get some poetic peace.

The second time is after that poet takes the MIC and those Words are spoken or read,
so here I am, releasing my Words, getting peace, until the next poetic thought enters my head!

Little Africa

Let me take you back in time and provide you with some knowledge.   I will tell you of a place you will not hear about while attending college.

The time was 1870 to 1921, for your historical notation, the north side of Tulsa, Oklahoma is the actual recorded location.

North Tulsa was called, "Little Africa," as this name marked praise.   The most affluent black community in America, the witnesses were amazed.

Jim Crow laws created all-black communities, we cannot deny it, and right down racial lines, was how the United States was divided.

Tulsa, Oklahoma was separated by the Arkansas River but not equal by any tale.   The white side was not nearly as prosperous while the black community completely excelled.

Little Africa contained black doctors, politicians, oil barons, and many PHD's, all black businesses, farmers, schools, and many black attorneys.

Black owned restaurants, grocery stores, libraries, movie theaters, and places to sleep,
so many prospering businesses that Greenwood Avenue was called Black Wall Street.

Yes, Black Wall Street because that is just how much money flowed.

I am not making this up, it is researched, and this is the
truth history holds.
Nepotism kept money circulating within this community
even for loans.
Everyone purchased from their neighbors which caused
the money to come back home.

Brotherly love and altruism were practiced while crime
was very low. Morals were taught to all and children
actually did what they were told.

Neighbors volunteered to help other neighbors in times
of trouble, and city families normally had five children
while farming families had about double.

White coal miners came to North Tulsa to work seventy-
two hour long shifts as well. So, they too helped the
pockets of these black businesses to swell.

In the 1800's, Little Africa had its own transportation
system to assist them all. Blacks kept to themselves and
took care of each other so no citizen would fall.

From Greenwood Avenue, to Archer, and Pine streets life
was prosperous and grand, and if you take the first
letters of those streets, G.A.P., you will see that is where
they got the name for the GAP Band.
By 1921 there were over one hundred black millionaires;
six even owned airplanes.
Black Wall Street was thriving and looking for more
financial gains.

On the south side many whites lived below the poverty
line, and white service men returning from World War I,
also fell on hard times.

"So, what happened to Little Africa?" one may say,
well, the Klu Klux Klan decided they were going to take
all that prosperity away.

On the first of June 1921, envy, greed, and jealousy took
control,
and a Black Holocaust in America was about to unfold.

This race riot was one of the most violent ever carried
out on American people.
It was the largest massacre of non-military Americans in
history with no recorded equal.

Within hours, thirty-six black owned businesses
destroyed on the north side of town.
Three thousand men, women, and children dead, and
hundreds could not be found.

Over 600 buildings destroyed, looted, and no longer
around. Hundreds of homes lit up the skies as they
burned right to the ground.
Meanwhile, good white Christian families just watched
and stood around, witnesses to the KKK killing anyone
whose skin color was brown.

Little Africa was unlawfully lynched as this massacre
went on for seventy-two hours and from yard to yard,
until the white sheriff sent his black deputy to call up the
State's National Guard.

The National Guard came to prevent the loss of more
innocent lives because death is what they saw,
and the first order of business was to establish and
enforce Martial Law.

They stopped the killings, aerial bombings, disarmed, and sent the Klan home, while doing their jobs.
They failed to save hundreds of business, dozens of grocery stores, churches, and restaurants, hundreds of homes and farms, two movie theaters, banks, schools, pawn shops, jewelry stores, and even a hospital laid in the wake of that hateful and angry mob.

Restitutions never happened, insurance claims dishonored, and black voices were silenced.
Mass graves around the city hid this act of complete and senseless violence.

Impacts, today African Americans have little nepotism and we have lost most of our financial power.
We seldom support each other and our money leaves the community within a couple of hours.

Consider this your history lesson for today and do not underestimate your economic might.
If you do not honor and protect what you have, it could be gone over night.

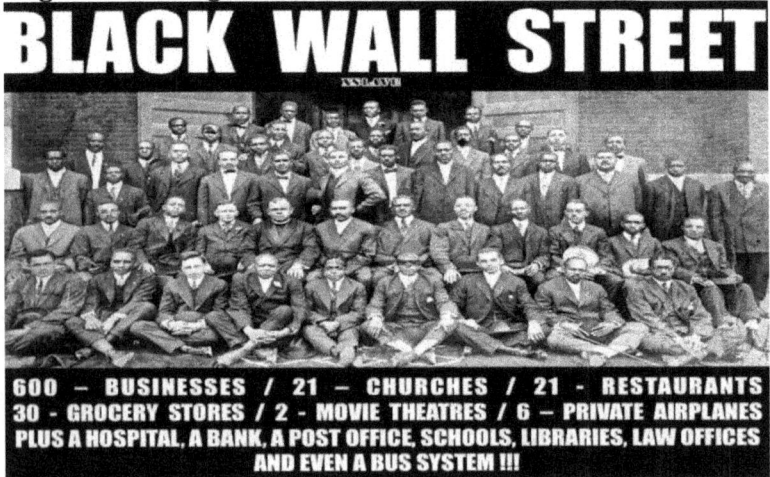

BLACK WALL STREET

600 – BUSINESSES / 21 – CHURCHES / 21 - RESTAURANTS
30 - GROCERY STORES / 2 - MOVIE THEATRES / 6 – PRIVATE AIRPLANES
PLUS A HOSPITAL, A BANK, A POST OFFICE, SCHOOLS, LIBRARIES, LAW OFFICES
AND EVEN A BUS SYSTEM !!!

THE HEART OF A MILITARY LEADER

I am the KING!

Do you actually know the truth about your history?
I mean, do you know his story while your past is still
a mystery?

Well, have you ever actually studied for yourself,
or are you living off someone else?

Just in case you did not know, I am a descendant of Kings.
I do not care what you were told!

You cannot believe everything taught to you
in school.
Many teachers and books are inaccurate, or they hide
the truth, which is not cool.

In 1492, Columbus did sail and land; that part is true,
but actually he was lost, killed many Caribbean natives,
and started the slave trade before he was through.

Our founding fathers wrote, "All men are created equal,"
but half of them owned slaves, and they mistreated a lot
of nonwhite people.

Thomas Jefferson worked the Louisiana Purchase, what
a deal he made,
but Native Americans owned the land, so why did
the French get paid?

Back in the day, minorities served freely on the
Republican Party's team,
while the Democrats were full of racists who helped
birth the Klan's dream.

THE HEART OF A MILITARY LEADER

Woodrow Wilson was a white supremacist at
Princeton, back in 1902.
As President, he set blacks back one hundred years, but that
is something else teachers neglected to tell you.

Knowledge can be one of the best friends you could
ever have had.
Walking around ignorant is ridiculous and extremely sad.

The fear they have of me dates back before they started
counting the days.
When I ruled this world they called it the Dark Age.

So, study your history as that should be one of your main
directives.
Now, let me address another audience and run down history
from a different prospective.

While I was king, I welcomed you into my land openly and
blindly.

Then you stabbed me in the back, so please do not remind me!

You stole me from my homeland while you were on your
crime spree.

You forced me to work your lands as you prospered so
handsomely.

You taught me lies, which I accepted whole heartedly.

You raped my women for years so now even your
blood runs through my seed,

but look at that Black Queen walking and living so boldly!

THE HEART OF A MILITARY LEADER

Thanks for leading me back to my God because you realized He also loves me.

Then I prayed to God, who set me free from your tyranny.

After slavery, your justice was hanging black men in public from trees,

but I have been through slavery so that does not define me!

I deal with your racism, and I refuse to let that bind me!

I even had to sue you in court for my right to get an equal opportunity.

I pray to God for love and to forgive, so I can live more divinely,

but do not push me because all that anger is not completely behind me.

We can work together; lead this world, so we can all live freely,

but just remember we are equals, so come brother walk beside me!

The First Cowboy

Hello everyone. It is time for another of Mr. Speaker's history lessons.
Listen up because I will give you the facts and the truth, so there will be no guessing.

During slavery, black men were called many derogatory names, and treated like toys.
They were considered property, not men, as most of the names ended with the word boy.

Names such as houseboy, field-boy, and even cowboy where names they answered to.
They were called other derogatory names, but about that, I should not have to tell you.

Many Africans lived in villages where they raised and cared for animals in flocks everyday.
As slaves they already knew how to raise live stock, and watch over them as they grazed.

Indians and Mexicans taught Blacks how to rope cattle, and ride horses as together they served.
Blacks taught them how to tend to animals in large flocks or herds.

Some of the first cowboys were former slaves, and they made being a cowboy appealing to all.
Herding cattle was big business, and you had to be trained to move cattle to the market and auction halls.

THE HEART OF A MILITARY LEADER

History fails to write about the first black cowboys, which is not new or strange.
Who else do you think was homeless, and roaming around on the open range?

Ponder this as you think over the things I say, and play with it in your mind like a toy.
During this time, no self-respecting white man would ever let someone call him boy.

Those white cowboys you see in movies, and read all about,
well many originally learned at the feet of great black men, and that is no doubt.

Great black cowboys like Bill Pickett, Jim Perry, Ben Hodges, and Blas Payne,
they were known to be some of the finest cowboys to ever ride the open range.

Cowgirls like Mary Ellen Pleasant, Biddy Mason, and Aunt Clara Brown.
Lead by, "Stagecoach" Mary Fields, how else do you think the U.S. mail got from town to town?

Charley Glass, Edward Rose, Moses "Black" Harris, John Stewart, and Greenbury Logan all passed the test.
Willie Simms, Cherokee Bill, Jesse Stahl, George Monroe, and William Robinson were some of the finest riders on that, "Pony Express."

The list is just too long, but they should be remembered as they helped pave our way west.
When it came to herding cattle, hands down, these guys were known to be the best.

Cowboys even helped with the Underground Railroad as slaves escaped to freedom.
Cowboys like my great, great, great, great grandfather William Lambert from Detroit, cannot wait to meet him.

Europeans invaded Africa, and stole many things to include knowledge and education,
so that pattern was repeated over and over not just there, but in many other locations.

Even today the black man is copied and emulated by many perpetrators.
People want to pimp their rides, speak slang, and change their clothes just to emulate us.

Do not worry; you can keep all the fashion and things you have jacked.
Everyone knows where you got your style, and without it you would be wack.

Just be cool as you copy me, no need to fight, no need for assault and battery.
Deep down you know you like me because, "Imitation is the best form of flattery."

Buffalo Soldiers

Born in battle, named by their Indian foes,
served this country well, though many do not know.

Buffalo Soldiers is what they were named,
because they helped clear and settle the open range.

They also served in the Revolutionary War and that is no doubt,
and they served during the Civil War for the North and the South.

The Union Army promised them freedom if they served,
while the confederates forced them to duty, but kept them in the reserve.

From Oklahoma, to Kansas, Arizona, New Mexico, and Texas they gave settlers peace of mind.
The Ninth and Tenth Calvary along with the Twenty-fourth and Twenty-fifth Infantry are where many were assigned.

They also fought bravely in Cuba, but that is not what Teddy Roosevelt would say.
Some people really did not like black Soldiers back in the day.

General Custer refused to command Buffalo Soldiers because he had no vision.
Later he got his command massacred because of other poor decisions.
No matter the challenge they served, but with discrimination they had a head on collision.

They fought aerial fire balloon bombs set by the Japanese during World War II.
These bombs were floated in the jet stream, and over the west coast is where they blew.

Buffalo Soldiers fought gallantly until all the United State's enemies were defeated,
but by fellow white Soldiers they were still mistreated.

Even captured German Soldiers, while prisoners of war, were treated better than our own Buffalo Soldiers whose rights were ignored.

While America was fighting oppression and Nazis with military formation,
they were still practicing segregation, teaching racism, and breeding discrimination.

That did not stop Buffalo Soldiers back in the day,
and it has not hindered other service personnel who helped pave the way.

Twenty-three Buffalo Soldiers earned the Congressional Medal of Honor for their services.
One female, Cathy Williams, disguised herself to serve; see you may not have learned this.

They had cavalry formations and multiple units of fighting infantry.
From November 1862 Buffalo Soldiers sacrificed, fought, and died because freedom is not free.

THE HEART OF A MILITARY LEADER

In the 1950's the United States military integrated ending
this glorious tradition of service;
forced to join all white units caused everyone to be a bit
nervous.

Bonds were formed as the United States military forged
ahead.
Soldiers realized we all fought for freedom and we all
bled red.

We still have a long way to go as equality, justice, and
harmony we chase.
Look real close and you will see the spirit of a Buffalo
Soldier in my face!

THE HEART OF A MILITARY LEADER

Momma I Listened

Momma I listened when you spoke, I listened when you yelled,
and I even listened when you cried.

Momma I listened when you spanked me, worked
long hours, and as you thanked God for everything.

Momma, I listened when you would not let me fail;
when you refused to let me quit.

I also listened when you would not accept that I was
educationally slow, and I listened as you smiled while I
received my master's degree.

Momma I listened to you when others would not.
I listened to you when others hurt you.

I also listened to you as you sang, and as you showed me
how to pray as you taught Sunday school.

Momma I really listened, as you went to work early every day,
and as we never missed church; as you taught me right from
wrong and as you showed me tough love. Momma I listened.

Momma, I wrote this for you and others to see,
because I listened to you now hundreds and hundreds
listen to me!

Now look at what listening to you has done for me.
Momma, I listened.

The Author

James F. Sears, Jr. was born on June 21st to Catherine and James Sears in Louisville, Kentucky where he grew up playing football, soccer, and running track while possessing a passion for basketball. James graduated from Louisville Male High School in 1985 and he is one of the few individuals who is a fan of both the University of Louisville and the University of Kentucky sports programs. He initially enlisted into the Kentucky National Guard as a 76W/Petroleum Truck Driver in 1985 while attending Western Kentucky University (WKU).

While at WKU, James served in the Kentucky National Guard and he received a commission as a Second Lieutenant into the United States Army.

He served in the U.S. Army Reserves in Louisville, KY until he graduated from WKU with a bachelors of science in business administration and reported for active duty. Additionally, while at WKU, James was a member of the Amazing Tones of Joy Gospel Choir, WKU Senior ROTC program, served as residence assistant for two years, became a member of Kappa Alpha Psi Fraternity Inc., and worked as a manager at a local McDonalds.

James' first active duty assignment was at Fort Sill, OK where he completed the Field Artillery Officer Basic and Gunnery Courses, was assigned to the 2nd Battalion (BN) 17th Field Artillery (FA) and deployed immediately to Saudi Arabia in support of Operations Desert Shield\Storm. In 1992, James graduated from the Quartermaster Branch Qualification Course, Fort Lee, VA which qualified him as a logistical officer and then he was assigned to 2nd BN 18th FA, Fort Sill, where he served as the Battalion Ammunition Platoon Leader and Battalion S4 completing two rotations to the National Training Center, located at Fort Irwin, California.

In 1995, James graduated from the Combined Logistics Officer Advance Course at Fort Lee, VA and was assigned to the 2nd Infantry Division Support Command (DISCOM), Republic of Korea (Camp Casey). There he served as the DISCOM S1 (Personnel Officer) and later he took command of Bravo (Maintenance) Company, 2nd Forward Support Battalion, 2nd Infantry Division (Camp Hovey).

In 1997, James returned to Fort Lee, VA where he taught logistics to hundreds of commissioned and warrant officers and he later served as the Regimental Adjutant for the 46th Quartermaster General Major General Hawthorne L. Proctor.

In 2001, after simultaneously graduating from Central Michigan University with a Masters of Science and Administration in Human Resource Management and the Command and General Staff College, (CGSC), Fort Leavenworth, KS, James was assigned to the 3rd Infantry Division, DISCOM, Fort Stewart, GA. While at Fort Stewart, James served as the DISCOM S4, Support Operations Officer for 703rd Main Support Battalion and DISCOM Support Operations Officer. In 2003, he deployed in support of Operation Iraqi Freedom where he planned the logistical operations which enabled the 3rd Infantry Division to successfully attack and defeat the Iraqi Army and set the conditions for regime change in Iraq.

James was then assigned as the Transformation Team Chief, United States Forces Command (FORSCOM) G4 during the summer of 2004. In 2005, he was selected to command the 840th Deployment and Distribution Support Battalion (SDDC) Balad, Iraq where he was responsible for the redeployment of tactical units from Iraq, port operations, and tactical container management. While on his third combat tour in Iraq, James discovered poetry was a very effective way to relieve and release the stress of leading troops in combat. Born in battle, Mr. Speaker officially started writing poetry while stationed in Balad, Iraq 2007 but he has been gathering knowledge for his poetry for as long as he can remember.

After command, James was assigned as the Chief, Joint Petroleum Officer, United States European Command, (EUCOM) Stuttgart Germany where he managed millions of gallons of fuel in Europe, Northern Iraq, and Northern Afghanistan. He was additionally responsible for Joint Ammunition and Strategic Contacting operations.

Mr. Speaker is one of the founding members of Vox Imperium Poetry Crew from Stuttgart, Germany, which means "word control" in Latin. The Vox crew hosted poetry events and performed all over Germany and produced one poetry CD before they started to move to other military locations.

James Sears was then assigned as the Chief of Plans and Operations Branch, Joint and Army Experimentation Division (JAED), Concepts Development & Learning Directorate (CDLD) Army Capabilities Integration Center (ARCIC), TRADOC, Fort Eustis. While in Virginia, Mr. Speaker hosted several poetry readings and he has featured at the Nuyorican Poet's Café and several locations in Virginia and North Carolina. Additionally, James worked as an adjunct professor at Saint Leo University teaching Human Resource Management and Business Management. James is a life member of Kappa Alpha Psi Fraternity Inc., and an active alumni member. He is also an active member in a professional military mentoring organization called the ROCKS Inc.

Poetically, James has produced a Vox Imperium Crew CD in 2010 and a Kappa Alpha PSI Poetry and Chants CD in 2011 and he is currently working on two additional poetry CD projects. James or Mr. Speaker is a member of the Virginia Poetry Society, he has served as a host for Poetic Expression at Queen's Way Soul Café, The House of Consciousness, Barnes and Noble Open Mic Fridays, and Co-Host a weekly poetry blog talk radio show with C Bravo of C Bravo Productions. You can join them by simply dialing 1-646-478-5603 every Wednesday at 7pm Eastern Standard Time.

Additional with C. Bravo Productions, James has taken scores of poets from Virginia and North Carolina to New York City to perform at the Nuyorican Poetry Café and other venues in New York City.

Currently assigned at the Pentagon, James has served this country for over 24 years and he has earned two Bronze Star Medals, a host of other awards, completed three combat tours, while successfully commanding Soldiers at two different levels. He has two beautiful daughters Sydnee and Jaila Sears and he is very thankful to you for purchasing his first book and appreciates your support.